TOME OF

HERALDIC

EXCELLENCE

The Knightly Order

Of the Fiat Lux

Written and edited by

His Grace Lord Karl Strohminger, Ph.D

Published by

The Knightly Order of the Fiat Lux

January 13, 2014

Special thanks to contributors:

His Grace Lord Michael Black

Lord Paul Satenstein

Sir Gene Kinney

Tome of Heraldic Excellence

Section I: Knight Herald's Duties

It's been said that the chapter Knight Herald is often the primary manager of a chapter. While the Grand Knight Beacon is undeniably in charge, and purposely most all decisions rest on his shoulders, it is the Herald who enacts the chapter's policies in many instances. One could almost think of the chapter Herald as the chief of staff to the GKB's presidency. More accurately however, the term "field director" is appropriate. In addition, the Herald has the following primary duties: membership recruitment, membership development, chapter quality performance, chapter martial activities, and risk management. A knight interested in helping make a chapter all it can be, but uninterested in the mantle of leadership or command, is a great candidate for herald. So is a knight who wants to one day be a GKB, but perhaps feels like he needs some on-the-job training. The following list of task and functions is by no means the complete list of possible duties, it is only the beginning. A Grand Knight Beacon may add or subtract from these duties as he sees fit within policy. Yep, the "and all other duties as assigned" clause applies.

Membership Development

There are several aspects of membership development a Knight Herald need be concerned with, including recruitment, rank advancement, Feats of Character and Combat, and record keeping.

It has been often said that "as long as we're recruiting, nothing else matters. The day we stop recruiting, nothing else matters". Recruitment is the life blood of the Fiat Lux. With more members, we raise more money for those in need. With more members, we perform more service hours for agencies needing our help. With more members, we make our communities a better place. For this reason, all members are charged with recruitment. "Each one, teach one", if you will. But it is the Herald who has the formal responsibility for this function. Often, chapters see the Herald in the role of martial commander, and only this role. Sadly, often Heralds themselves make the same mistake. In fact, the martial duties are secondary to membership development. For this reason, membership development comes before martial direction in this Tomb.

Tasks for Membership Recruitment expected of a successful Knight Herald:

- Conduct an annual membership drive in cooperation with the Lord Herald of the National Privy Council, or conduct a local drive if no national campaign is available. Membership drives can take many forms:
- *Incentive Campaign*: reward members with an incentive for different membership metrics, such as number of guests at an event, number of possible recruits at a meeting/event, number of new squires recruited, etc. Incentives can be physical, such as a new sword or surcoat, financial such as next year's dues or ABM fee paid, or honorary, such as a title or honorific. In an incentive campaign, any member can reach the goal.
- *Contest Campaign*: similar to the incentive campaign, but only one knight, or team, can win the prizes by leading the metric.
- *Universal Campaign*: This campaign would be the most successful, but is a top down, mandatory approach, and may engender some resentment from members. A universal campaign basically requires every member to perform a task related to recruitment, such as invite potential members to a dinner, recruit a squire, knight one new member, etc. This would certainly build membership, but also runs the risk of reducing the quality of recruits. This theme is recommended for small chapters only.
- *Voluntary Campaign*: In a voluntary campaign, results will be mixed, but possibly the quality of recruits will increase. Offer no incentives, require no action, but make

a big deal, a HUGE deal, over the recruitment actions of any member. Recognize them at Conclaves and events, post the recruitment story on the Forums or social media, etc. Everyone likes a good "attaboy" in public. In a voluntary campaign, and indeed, in any recruitment campaign, it is crucial for the Herald to lead by example.

Tips for a successful recruitment campaign:

- **Develop a recruitment team (membership committee) and formulate a goal.** Work together with your Conclave to establish a team goal and individual goals, and be sure to assign specific responsibilities and completion dates. Make sure the goal is reasonable and attainable while still challenging. While seeking new members, be sure someone on the team works on member retention or getting previous members to renew or re-obtain good standing.

- **Target potential members** Define your objective (what you want to accomplish), your strategy (a plan of action to achieve what you want to accomplish), and your methods (the tactics you are going to use to implement your plan) to target potential members effectively. Consider recruiting members at medieval events, at public exhibitions, via social media, at the coffee shop, anywhere men of quality gather, and by asking people to join, etc. Pick strategies and methods that will fit your individual strengths, comfort level, budget, time, and expertise.

- **Make everyone feel welcome.** Develop a plan for teaching new members about KOFL and for making them feel as though they are part of the organization. A regular orientation evening (perhaps a dinner) with new and old members is an effective way to introduce new members. Suggest that all members check out the KOFL Membership Handbook and website. It's a great way for new members to learn about KOFL and for long-time members to gain a fresh look at their association.

- **Include Everyone.** Make your recruitment plan reflect the diversity of your community. Make sure that the materials you produce take into account the background and interests of those you are targeting to join, and that they are not excessively medieval in nature.

- **<u>Sell the value of KOFL membership.</u>** Recruiting new members goes hand-in-hand with making sure they find value in KOFL. Keep members motivated through on-going communication, opportunities to volunteer, and recognition. Emphasize to new members what they get for their membership dues; for example, martial training, opportunity to serve others, personal growth, belonging, newsletters, and association with other fine men., However, **<u>the number one benefit that KOFL members receive from membership is the ability to help their own community.</u>**

- **<u>Collaborate with and learn from others.</u>** People like to join organizations that make a difference in the lives of others, are educational and beneficial to the community, allow them to network with other people, and provide opportunities to have fun. Tap into the expertise of individual members and let them showcase their talents through local activities. An example may be a fight demonstration at a local men's group like the Moose Lodge or even a Sunday church men's group. The <u>KOFL Membership Handbook</u> has a great presentation on the Armor of God; consider calling a minister and offer to put it on for his church groups for free! They will JUMP at the chance.

- **<u>Assist with learning initiatives.</u>** Contact your local schools and offer any number of KOFL presentations for their classes, after-school programs, school fairs, etc. Always, provide each attending student a brochure and invite him to check out the website. If the student is 18 or older, get HIS email and invite him back. Today's youth are tomorrow's members.

- **<u>Implement your chapter's membership recruitment and retention plan.</u>** Plans are worthless unless they are put into practice. Be sure to schedule your recruitment and retention activities throughout the year, and particularly at events such as RenFaires and other medieval events. Assign a specific person to be in charge of coordinating the different events, but involve all of your members. Every event your chapter holds is a chance to have more people join, so always have your sign-up sheets and information ready!

- **<u>Don't forget to reach out to past members.</u>** We've seen it many times. For one reason or other, a member falls by the way side. After a couple months, they are embarrassed at dropping off the face of the world, and then just don't come back. Reach out to each and every one of these members *at least* once a year, ensure them they are missed, loved and welcomed back. Ask them what about the Fiat Lux they like most, and invite them to an event featuring that aspect! Ask them if there were any problems, then solve them!

- **Evaluate and adjust accordingly.** Continuously seek feedback from team members on issues such as how many new members they are recruiting, how they are helping these new members acclimate to KOFL and get involved, and how many members are staying active. Regardless of whether the evaluation is done through a formal survey or informal communication, it should be systematic, recorded and used to adjust and improve the membership plan's strategy.

- Follow-up. Check back frequently with any member who has taken a squire recently, and ensure progress towards knighthood is happening. Feel free to ask the new squire about his experiences and needs. Offer help.

- Report to your Conclave successes and failures in recruitment at every meeting.

Tasks for Rank Advancement Management for a successful Knight Herald

- Survey your chapter membership and log each member's rank.

- Familiarize yourself with all rank requirements, procedures and opportunities as outlined in the KOFL Membership Handbook.

- Inquire of your members as to their goals and desires pertaining to rank advancement. You may find many do not understand the value of advancement, nor understand the process. Counsel any member interested in process and value. Educate everyone else too!

- Celebrate all rank advancements in your chapter in a public and big way. Parties, dinners and presents are not inappropriate. Suggest to a member's original sponsoring knight that he may wish to send a small gift or letter of congratulations. You may even secure that knight's support in encouraging the stalled member to take the next Feat!

- Inform the GKB of your chapter, and an appropriate Heartsman, when a squire is ready to advance in rank. Assist the Heartsman with properly coordinating the trials of knighthood, the Feat of Character or combat, and the Court of Accolades.

Tasks for Profile Management

- Simply put, the chapter Knight Herald is charged with ensuring all chapter members have an up-to-date profile on record. Review and audit these records at least quarterly.

Chapter Duties

As a member of a Chapter Conclave, a Knight Herald has a couple duties related to quality chapter management, mainly pertaining to paperwork and record keeping.

Tasks for a successful Knight Herald in ensuring chapter quality

- Review any annual program from the ONT related to chapter quality (I.E. Chapter of Distinction or Destruction) and develop a plan to meet those metrics in coordination and participation with other officers.

- Ensure the ONT paperwork is reviewed by your chapter, properly authorized, and returned to the ONT in a timely manner.

- Review the various line items in the ONT chapter quality assurance program at all Conclaves to review status and progress.

- Return the appropriate forms to the ONT to ensure your chapter receives appropriate recognition.

- Encourage all of your chapter members to participate and embrace the ONT program of chapter quality assurance.

- If your chapter has a chapter heraldic device, the knight herald is charged with maintaining said devices, and to ensure they meet Articles of Organization requirements.

- The Knight Herald oversees the chapter equipment to include weapons, artifacts, medical gear, martial equipment, etc. He may, with GKB permission, appoint a Quartermaster, or just handle the task alone. A list of goods and gear should be kept up to date, and made available to any chapter member or the ONT upon request.

- Keep chapter gear in a serviceable and safe condition.

Martial Duties

Without a doubt, it is the martial expectations of a Knight Herald that are the most well known, the most visible, and from which most heralds derive the most satisfaction. While not the herald's most important duty, let none minimize the importance of a solid martial program. Chapter Knight Heralds are called upon to perform weapon and armor safety and compliance checks, maintaining a safe lyst field, overseeing all chapter medic operations, selecting and training line judges and lyst marshals, and ensuring chapter compliance with all official Rules of the Lyst. These are serious tasks, and require the most serious commitment to ensure safety is first, every swing of every sword!

Tasks of a martial nature required of a successful Knight Herald

- Safety is the crucial aspect of the herald function. As we swing items at each other with considerable force, it is VITALLY important that each and every weapon, be it a sword, axe, mace, flail, spear, shield or other item, meet each and every standard as proscribed by the Rules of the Lyst TO THE LETTER. To that end, a Knight Herald MUST be intimately familiar with the entire current version of the Rules of the Lyst. Know each and every standard, rule or proscription in the book to a mnemonic certainty. It is just as important that all armor is just as safe.

- Review the Rules of the Lyst often, at least bi-monthly.

- Ensure all weapons, soft, wood or steel, are in compliance with the ROTL by visually and tactically inspecting them. Look for burs, gouges, proper blunts and tips, and metal type with live steels. For boffers, look for solid unbroken cores, tight tape and pommels, no "dog ears" on tape and fabric, sufficient "give' to the padding to absorb the impact and secure pommels.

- Check shields for protruding screws and bolts, splinters, burs or other imperfections that may cause injuries, proper shield coverings, solid cores, and appropriate handles and straps, unbroken and sufficient for the user.

- Check that all male fighters are properly equipped in every martial engagement. Check that live steel or wood sword fighters are properly geared according to the ROTL.

- Check and ensure safe compliance with all other weapons as needed ala the ROTL. Again, know it inside and out.

- Ensure any and all lyst fields are safe according to ROTL standards.

- A Chapter Knight Herald is automatically THE senior Lyst Marshal of his chapter, and as such, oversees the entire marshal corp. At any time, a KH may take his chapter's lyst field as his own, and marshal it. However, a KH MAY NOT overrule the on-duty lyst marshal on any individual call. He may relieve a marshal of duty, but does not have appeal authority on lyst calls not made himself.

- Knights Herald are charged with ensuring Order medic regulations are followed to the letter, to include any medic regulations of the ROTL, the ONT or the Articles of Organization, local, state and federal regulations, and any additional chapter rules and procedures that apply.

- Ensure your chapter has a sufficient list of trained medics available.

- Work with the medic staff to ensure fighters are medically able to participate. A KH may support a medic "unfit" call, but may not overrule it to the permissive side. For instance, if a medic says Sir Dogooder is unfit to fight due to an injury, the KH may not then permit the participation. However, the KH may pull a fighter when the medic does not.

- Ensure a sufficient corps of trained lyst marshals and line judges are readily available to your chapter by recruiting members and chapter friends to learn the standards and take the training for both roles.

- Train lyst marshals and line judges as needed.

- Maintain records of medics, injuries and incidents.

- Maintain records of line judges and lyst marshals.

Order Duties

Just as the Knight Herald helps ensure a chapter runs properly, so too does he help the ONT function as needed. Primarily, this takes the form of helping as needed at national martial events, and assisting the Lord Herald with his duties. For instance, some Lords Herald ask their Knights Herald to serve on a standing roundtable for herald policies and review. Additionally, all heralds are often called to help marshal and judge at the Tournament of Light or the Tournament of the Phoenix. Though not required, a sharp Knight Herald may offer his services while visiting other chapter martial events too.

- A standing herald roundtable helps eliminate disparate and inconsistent understandings and interpretations of the ROTL. For instance, exactly what does "or other suitable material" mean? In, 2013, a standing herald roundtable was instrumental in helping formulate a concussion awareness policy and program as mandated by our insurance provider.

Sir Barton Jones is tended to by Lyst Marshal Sir James Morasso after a skull jarring strike to the helmet. Fortunately, Sir James had ensured all armor standards were maintained and no injuries occurred. SAFETY IS HERALDIC JOB ONE! Lord Karl Strohminger (other fighter), Sir Christopher Babin, Sir Dieter Stoelting, and Sir Franklin Fite look on.

Section II: Lord Herald Duties

A Supreme Grand Knight Beacon, per the Articles of Organization, is free to appoint privy council ministers, called "Lords (Office)", to assist with the management of the Order. This system is based heavily on King Henry the Eighth's administration. It is important here to reiterate an often overlooked point. The Order exists to serve the needs of others. This service takes many forms, as "a life of honor begins, is, and ends in service". While the chapters primarily are charged with serving external audiences, such as families, communities, and charities, the Office of the National Trustee has an INTERNAL focus. It exists to serve the Order's needs. This cannot be overstated. When the ONT takes a leadership role in corporate and organizational responsibilities, the chapters, and hence, the members themselves, are freed from this burden and able to focus on more important matters, like raising money for kids!

Although not required to appoint a Lord Herald, as of 2013, no Supreme Grand Knight Beacon has failed to do so. This is for a very good reason, the LH is vital to a smooth functioning ONT. In many ways, the LH is a busier, more in depth, and more critical office than his brethren Lords such as the Chamberlain, Exchequer and Steward. Although incapable of forming policy, the Herald, similar to his chapter analogue, enacts the SGKB's will, along with the rest of the privy council. No other privy council office, save perhaps the Lord Chamberlain, has as many delineated and defined duties as the LH. These duties include: producing the Tournament of Light, managing the Order's insurance needs, approving lyst marshals and medics, serving as the Order senior lyst marshal, coordinating schedules by publishing and marketing all Order and chapter events, overseeing the Tournament of the Phoenix, serving as the Annual Business Meeting Master-at-arms, encouraging brotherhood development, keeping the Order heraldry, overseeing medical policies such as the Concussion Policy, serving on the Privy Council, overseeing the chapter quality evaluation process and maintaining many records. It should be noted that as of 2013, the duties of maintaining the Order *master roster* have been reassigned to the Lord Chamberlain, but a SGKB may reverse that decision in future administrations. Therefore, those duties will also be described in this Tomb.

Lord Paul Satenstein, 201?, Lord Herald, performing a [?] field safety check at the Autur[?] Jubilee, Rowan County, NC

The Tournament of Light

The Tournament of Light is the Order's premiere martial event. With very few years' exceptions, the Order has held a Tournament of Light every year. Some of these tournaments have been quite grand, with scores of attendees and dozens of competitors. Additionally, the overall winner of the TOL is the serving Order Champion until the next TOL is held. For these reasons, and because it's scrupulous, the Lord Herald's primary responsibility any given year is producing a quality TOL.

Tasks for Producing the Tournament of Light

- Early in the program year, secure a date, usually in the early Autumn, that does not conflict with Chapter events. The early Autumn time frame is not required, but is customary.
- Secure a location for the tournament as soon as feasible. Consider facility needs such as convenient location for as many members as possible, rest room facilities, space, safety and atmosphere. Suggestions include a local park, the Charlotte Commandary, martial arts studios, or a

private camp location. Even a member's home sometimes serves quite well.

- Set a budget for the event by conferring with the SGKB as to his expectations for the event's financial success. Customarily, the TOL's budget projects a 20% profit, with the net proceeds going to the ABM budget. However, anything is possible. Budgets should consider cost of awards, water and drink supplies, paper and office supply needs, marketing needs, travel fees for any required privy council member, catering or costs of meals, etc. Compile a list of expenses before settling on an admission fee. The admission fee may be a straight fee, or an ala carte fee charging for each event. (see below)

- Market the tournament as early in the program year as possible. Include in your marketing materials the fees for participation, a list of events, a list of awards and prizes, and any "sizzle" that excites attendees. Marketing options include, but are not limited too, Facebook and social media, the Forums, emails to members, flyers, etc. If the TOL is open to outside audiences, consider the forums and social media outlets of local LARPS (Live Action Role Play such as the SCA, SOLAR, Dagorhir, etc) and other medieval or HEMA (historical European martial arts such as Chivalry Sports Academy or EMAA).

- Recruit sufficient personnel to help with managing the event. Support personnel include marshals, cooks, medics, greeters, score keepers, etc. The chapter heralds are a good first place to recruit, but any Order member appropriately qualified may serve. Even non-Order members have been asked to help with catering, cooking and medical duties.

- Establish, with the advice and approval of the SGKB, any rules changes, additions, or particulars of the tournament.

For instance, in 2013, the new freestyle live steel rules often referred to as "The Coker Rules" were added to the official schedule. The 2013 staff also limited the official marshals to THREE individuals, ensuring a consistent subjective evaluation of the lyst. The LH is fairly free to adjust, determine, or decide how he will do the TOL, within the confines of the Rules of the Lyst.

- Collect all pre-admissions payments, perhaps offering a discount for pre-payment.
- Secure the food or catering operations BEFORE the event. Decide who will purchase food. Be prepared to do that yourself with event pre-payment monies.
- A month or so before the event: inquire to the membership if anyone will need time for a Court of Accolades. The TOL is one of the two most meaningful times for a dubbing, along with the ABM.
- One week before tournament: publish the final schedule of events to the members and attendees.
- Day of the Tournament: ensure awards, decorations, medical gear, loaner combat gear (if permissible), food, drinks, etc. all taken care of, on hand, and employed.
- Day of Tournament: greet every attendee and guest. Collect any unpaid fees and register attendees, combatants, and guests. Seed the brackets as fighters register.
- Day of Tournament: serve as senior lyst marshal. Be prepared to make lyst related calls and decisions all day long. If necessary, marshal a lyst yourself if the schedule allows.
- Day of Tournament: serve as master-of-ceremonies or recruit a good candidate for that role if it's not something you are comfortable doing. You may also wish to ask the SGKB what, if any, role he expects to play.

- Day of Tournament: ensure facility is properly cleaned, and closed down. Thank your attendees and staff.
- Day after Tournament: announce the winners.
  - Possible TOL events include: live steel lyst, soft sword lyst, "Coker" rules lyst, archery competition, field battles, non-standard rules lyst, single or double elimination brackets, team or chapter competitions, bardic contests, regalia inspections, and much more. The skies the limit!
  - Currently used titles include: Bard of Light, Victor of Light (7 PT Live Steel), Vanguard of Light (Chapter battles), Blademaster of Light (7 PT soft sword), Sagamour of Light (Coker rules), *Champion of Light* (overall champion and new Order Champion)
  - Scoring options may include raw scores (total points earned), total wins, or some weighted scoring of many factors.

The 2013 Tournament of Light "Coker Rules" Fighters; Sir Tracy Talley, Lord Paul Satenstein, Sir Barton Jones, Lord Stuart Nicholson, Sir Buck Holmes, His Grace Lord Michael Black and Man-at-arms Johnathon McCartney.

Order Insurance Policies

As our primary reason for carrying insurance is liability related to the lyst field, the Order senior martial officer, the LH, is responsible for liaising with our insurance provider. A SGKB may choose to handle this responsibility himself however.

Our current insurance carrier, as of 2014, is:

Agent: Sally Mansour

Terry L. Green & Associates, Inc.
P.O. Box 367
Snellville, GA 30078
Phone 678-205-8042
Fax 678-205-8043
Terry Green Insurance Services CA Ins. OE 39335
The underwriter is the United States Fire Insurance Company of Eatontown, NJ.

Tasks related to Insurance for the Lord Herald:

o   Maintain contact with Sally Mansour, or the agent of note, through the year.
o   Ensure the policy is renewed in a timely manner.
o   Assist the SGKB in adjudicating the "per member" cost for insurance. IE. How will the ONT pay the premium?
o   Provide insurance proofs for any chapter needs by coordinating with the agent.
o   Annually, research other carriers and agents for better rates.

Senior Lyst Marshal

The Lord Herald is the senior Order martial officer. Members may, and do, come to the Lord Herald often for his assistance in interpreting the Rules of the Lyst or other Order martial regulations. There are often significant differences in the interpretation or understanding of different aspects of the ROTL. For instance, just what does "or suitable material" mean? What is sufficient force? As the senior lyst officer, there are incumbent responsibilities therein.

Tasks for the Senior Lyst Officer:
o   Approve all applications for lyst marshal certification. (See later)
o   Advise and consult with Knights Herald on their lyst marshal and line judge training program. Ensure all chapters have adequate access to all Order marshal training materials.
o   Issue lyst marshal certification documents using any appropriate process the Lord Herald deems. IE on line testing, written test, ABM classes, subordinate testing, etc.
o   If appropriate (check with the SGKB), hold lyst marshal and line judge training classes at the ABM.
o   Assist in lyst marshalling any lyst field, if the local chapter herald wishes, at any martial event you attend.
o   KNOW KNOW KNOW the Rules of the Lyst verbatim.
o   Know the Coker rules.
o   Know or be familiar with non-standard or unusual martial activities in which the Order may participate. For instance, Dagorhir rules.
o   Approve all lyst and Order medics per appropriate Order process.
o   Publish National policies related to martial activities as instructed by the SGKB, the National Conclave, or other authorities. IE, Concussion Policy.
o   Similar to a Knight Herald, a LH may marshal a field, but may only assert his preeminence in an ONT lyst. In other words, a LH should not assume he may take center position in a chapter lyst field; to do so would be unseemly. Likewise, he does not have appeal authority for any lyst marshal or medic call based on the ROTL.

o   Maintain all records related to lyst marshals (including training), medics and other martial paperwork, to include incident reports.

Rules of the Lyst
Version 1.2

Order Event Scheduling

Obviously, Chapters are free to schedule events whenever they wish. However, as the Order grows, scheduling conflicts are inevitable. The Lord Herald can help alleviate some of the entanglements.

Tasks for Order Scheduling by the Lord Herald:

o   Check with the chapters often to inquire as to their upcoming events over 1, 2, 3 and 6 months.
o   Publish this information, with exciting write-ups, in Order social media such as the website, the Forums, Facebook, The Beacon, etc.
o   Consult and advice chapters on timing of events.
o   Help chapters promote their events to other chapters.
o   ATTEND chapter events when you can.

Annual Business Meeting, National Conclaves and the Privy Council

The Lord Herald is not in the line of succession, but due to the nature of his duties, is often the first person called to help a member with a question. As his unique insight into the needs of chapters and members, his participation in the National Conclave and Privy Council are paramount.

Tasks for the Lord Herald as an ONT Officer:

o   Advise and consult with the SGKB on all matters martial. Likewise, be available to the National Conclave as senior martial officer and consultant. The LH does NOT have a NC vote, but should attend all NC meetings to advise, consult, and report on all matters martial.

o   Report on matters of martial activity to the privy council officers as such matters impact their duties. For instance, if the Tournament of Light needs seed money for marketing, request such monies from the Lord Exchequer.

o   Serve as Master-at-arms for both the National Conclave and the Grand Conclave. Calculate quorum and report to the SGKB. Take roll of attendees AND call and mark all roll call votes. Guard the door(s) of either meeting if necessary for Order business. Call said meetings to order.

o   Oversee the Tournament of the Phoenix. Recruit sufficient staff to run the tournament. Usually, the TOP is a double elimination live and soft sword contest only. Award the Phoenix Blade and Phoenix pins to the appropriate member, after securing these legacy awards from the previous year's winners.

o   Collect all completed chapter quality review process forms (IE Chapter of Distinction) and evaluate the chapter's success. Report your findings to the SGKB and prepare awards for his presentation at ABM.

o   Issue subsequent year chapter quality review process commitment forms.

o   All other duties as assigned by SGKB or LC.

Heraldic Roundtable

As often the case in KOFL, an institution arose from need more than from any intentional planning. In 2013, the Lord Herald frequently called upon the Knights Herald for their advice and consulting for various issues such as armor requirements, head injuries management, insurance rates, and many other topics. By the end of the year, the Knights Herald were effectively operating as a standing crusade (roundtable) under the chairmanship of the Lord Herald. This impromptu committee was INSTRUMENTAL in a number of process improvements for the Order, and in fact, is responsible for this manual's content. A Lord Herald may wish to utilize himself of this committee, and is strongly encouraged to do so.

Tasks of the Heraldic Roundtable:
o   Advice the LH on ROTL interpretation or contradiction.
o   Assist the LH by advising on possible new process ideas. IE. New awards, ideas for the Chapter of Distinction, or changes to training.
o   Discuss and debate various armor and equipment changes, ideas, etc.
o   Help the LH in marketing and producing events.
o   ALL Knights Herald are on this committee by virtue of their election.

Brotherhood Development

The Lord Herald assists the Knights Herald in helping to recruit members, promote ranks, and develop men of character.

Tasks for Brotherhood Development:
o   Consult with and advise Knights Herald on matters of brotherhood development, such as

eligibility of members to be promoted, recruitment campaign ideas, Courts of Accolade, etc.

o   Inspect chapters at appropriate times (IE chapter visits, ABM, TOL, etc.) by holding a full regalia inspection.

o   KNOW KNOW KNOW the relevant sections of the Articles of Organization on membership and rank eligibility, Courts of Honor, and regalia/heraldry.

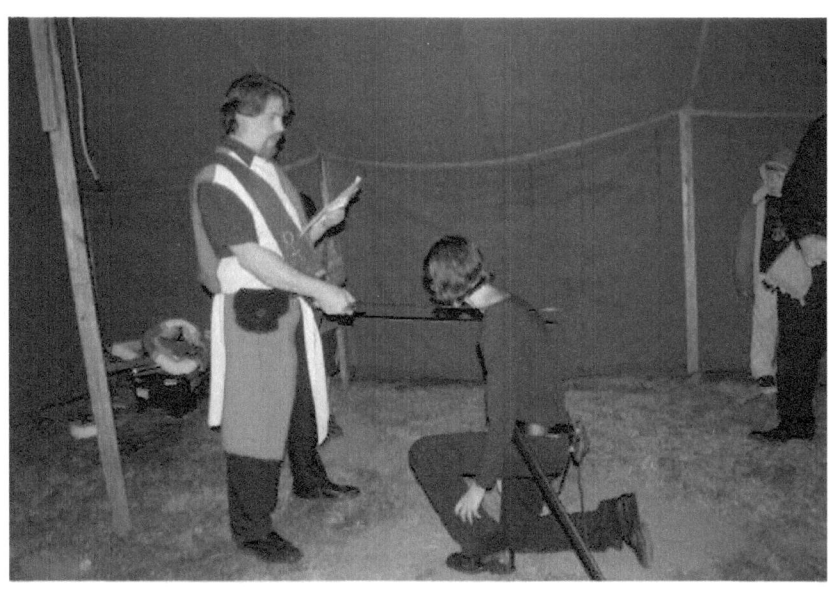

Lord Stuart Nicholson dubs an Invictus Chapter Knight

Section III: Training Materials

As the officer supervising field activities AND brotherhood development, training becomes a natural aspect of that role. This section includes many of the training materials and modules the Order uses in furtherance of its mission.

Lyst Marshal

It is important for any Herald to ensure an adequate supply of fully trained and effective lyst marshals. Many chapters choose to require all of their members be trained lyst marshals and require every member to take this training course annually. A word of caution on that approach however: ensure the member not only is trained but EFFECTIVE. The Order has seen inadequate and quite frankly poor performing marshals too many times. Consider criteria as to visual acuity, fairness, situational awareness, track record of good/bad calls, vocal strength and seniority when approving a member as a lyst marshal. No member should ever expect it is HIS right to be trained. Indeed, it is the marshal's duty to be selective.

As consistency in the lyst is a highly desired trait to ensure a safe, fair and accurate contest, the Lord Herald is charged with certifying all lyst marshal candidates and current marshals annually.

Lyst Marshal Training Process
- A member inquires as to training or is recruited by the Herald.
- Knight Herald requires the candidate to read the entire Rules of the Lyst and any and all ancillary martial publications (for instance, the Coker rules).
- When the candidate has read said publications, the knight herald quizzes him to his satisfaction.
- Candidate "shadows" the knight herald (or his designee herald/lyst marshal) for one event. The

event may be formal such as the Tournament of the Bronze Beast or Torchlight Tournament, or informal such as a chapter muster.

- Knight Herald reports candidate's readiness to the Lord Herald.
- Lord Herald conducts a fitness assessment (see below) and when satisfied, the candidate is issued an appropriate authorization card as a trained lyst marshal.
- ALL Order Lyst Marshals are required to undergo and complete the Lord Herald Lyst Marshal Certification Assessment annually. Certification documents will have an expiration date on them for this purpose.

KOFL Lyst Marshal Certification Card

Marshal's Name: **Sir Joseph Smith**
Date of Issue: **Jan 1, 2014**   Date of Exp.: **Dec. 31, 2014**
Issuing Lord Herald: **Lord John Doe**

Approved Fields: soft   steel   Coker   rattan
(circle appropriate)

Thou Shalt Scrupulously Perform Thy Noble Duties....

Authorizing Signature_____

Certification Requirements for KOFL Lyst Marshal

All members of the Knightly Order of the Fiat Lux that wish to become certified Lyst Marshals must complete this document and fulfill all of the following requirements annually. All Knights Herald are required to complete the training. *(Italicized items are required.)*

Name: _____ Date: _____

(Print Name)

1. *Know the rules of the Lyst for Soft Swords (Boffer)*

   K/LH _____

2. Know the rules of the Lyst for Rattan / Steel Swords

   K/LH _____

3. Know the rules of the Lyst for subjective matches/Coker rules

   K/LH _____

4. *Know the armor requirements for Soft Swords*

   K/LH _____

5. Know the armor requirements for Rattan / Steel Swords

   K/LH _____

6. Know the armor requirements for subjective matches/Coker

   rules   K/LH _____

7. *Know how to perform a weapons / armor check for all combats*

   K/LH _____

8. *Know the different commands and signals used in the Lyst*

   K/LH _____

9. *Know the different types of combats that take place within the Lyst*   K/LH   _____

10. *Know the scoring system for the Lyst*

   K/LH   _____

11. Know the scoring system for subjective matches/Coker rules

   K/LH   _____

12. *Complete the required concussion awareness training*

   K/LH   _____

13. *Demonstrate competence with all required martial paperwork*

   K/LH   _____

14. *Complete a training session with a Knight or Lord Herald*

   K/LH   _____

I _____, certify that the above applicant has completed to my satisfaction, all requirements needed to become a certified Lyst marshal for the Knightly Order of the Fiat Lux.

(Signature of applicant)

_____

(Signature of Knight Herald)

_____

Lord Herald's Approval_____

Please note with this system, a Lord Herald could certify a marshal for something less than full authority in the lyst. The italicized items are MANDATORY, but the others are optional. This way, a member could be certified to run a soft sword only lyst. The LH will place the letters NA for not applicable and his initials in the appropriate fields in these instances.

Official KOFL Concussion Policy

Pursuant to the Centers for Disease Control and our insurance provider's regulations the Knightly Order of the Fiat Lux has developed this policy to address the identification and proper handling of suspected head injury in all Order martial events.

Medical management of sports-related concussions is evolving. In recent years, there has been a significant amount of research into sports-related concussions in athletes. KOFL has established this protocol to provide education about concussions for martial staff and other personnel. This protocol outlines procedures for all participants to follow in managing head injuries, and outlines Order policy as it pertains to returning to lyst or martial activity after a concussion.

KOFL seeks to provide a safe return to activity for all participants after injury, particularly after a concussion. In order to effectively and consistently manage these injuries, procedures have been developed to aid in ensuring that concussed fighters are identified, treated and referred appropriately, receive appropriate follow-up medical care, and are fully recovered prior to returning to activity.

This protocol will be reviewed on a two year basis by the ONT, Order medics, and chapter heralds. Any changes or modifications will be reviewed and given to Order members and appropriate personnel in writing.

The Lord Herald of the Order shall be the person responsible for the implementation of these policies and procedures in coordination with chapter heralds, medics and all Order members. Chapter Heralds, lyst marshals, and all medics are required to review this policy every six months.

All live steel authorized members will complete an annual training module in which procedures for preventing and managing sports-related concussions are discussed. Heralds are required to instruct members and participants in form, technique and skills that minimize sports-related head injury and are directed to discourage and prohibit fighters from engaging in any unreasonably dangerous technique that endangers the health and safety of the Order and its members, including using a helmet and proper use of other sports equipment and weapons.

Participants who engage in unreasonably dangerous behavior while participating in martial activities will be subject to possible disciplinary consequences.

Training: The following personnel shall be required to participate in training in the prevention and recognition of sports-related head injuries: heralds, medics, lyst marshals, Grand Knight Beacons and all COKER rules fighters. Other Order members are strongly encouraged to receive training.

Training consists of taking the CDC on line webinar located at http://www.cdc.gov/concussion/headsup/online_training.html and review the written KOFL companion to include this policy and other information. The Lord Herald will maintain documentation of training completion and issue an appropriate authorization document to those who have completed the training. *NO PERSONNEL may manage or run an Order martial event without this authorization documentation.*

Documentation of history of head injuries, including concussions, is kept on file with the ONT with the completion of the consent form for each participant.

Pre-participation information concerning head injuries and concussions will be included in the consent form required of each participant and kept on file.

Removal from Athletic Activities due to Head Injury

Any fighter who, during a practice or competition, sustains a head injury or suspected concussion shall be removed from the practice or competition immediately and may not return to practice or competition that day. If necessary, family will be notified so the family may take the fighter to a medical provider for appropriate medical evaluation and treatment.

Any fighter removed for a possible head injury must provide medical documentation before being allowed to participate in practice or competition.

Medic Expectations

NO COMPETITION may occur without a documented medic on scene. Medics must have at least a current certification of their training of at least the level of American Red Cross First Aid training or higher. EMT, paramedic, nurse or physician levels are preferred. The on-scene Herald in charge will personally observe the documentation and ensure it is current.

"When in doubt, refer to the Medic on scene"

An understanding of the *Signs and Symptoms* are key. It is important to understand these because effective, quick treatment depends on early detection. In any situation where these symptoms are suspected, refer the injured party to the on-site medic immediately.

Signs and Symptoms

Thinking and remembering

- Not thinking clearly
- Feeling slowed down
- Not being able to concentrate
- Not being able to remember new information
- Delayed response to simple questions ('Who are you fighting', 'what's the score', etc)

- General confusion
- **Not feeling 'Right' most common symptom. Fighter will feel wrong but cannot articulate why.**

Physical
- **Headache extremely common. Can show up minutes after the injury**
- Fuzzy or blurry vision
- Nausea and vomiting
- Dizziness
- Sensitivity to light or noise
- Balance problems
- Feeling tired or having no energy

Emotional and mood
- Easily upset or angered
- Sad
- Nervous or anxious
- More emotional than usual

Sleep
Sleeping more than usual
Sleeping less than usual
Having a hard time falling asleep

The following are signs of a SERIOUS possible concussion and require transportation to a Hospital immediately:

A loss of consciousness lasting more than a minute

- **Repeated** vomiting
- Seizures

- Obvious difficulty with mental function or physical coordination

- Symptoms that worsen over time

- Anisocoria (Unequal Pupil Size)

If you are observing an incident in which you think a concussion might be possible, don't hesitate to have the individual evaluated. It doesn't hurt to have a medic check them out.

Because concussions can be difficult to identify, the following incidents may allow a medic to require a fighter to sit out (time out) while waiting to see if symptoms show up.

Any strike to the head that directly forces a fighter to his/her knees or lower.

Any strike to the head that directly results in the fighter losing consciousness. (Required "time out")

Any direct fall from a fully standing position where the head strikes a hard surface unimpeded (Eg, The CC Lyst Field beams).

A minimum of a 30 minute break from all activity is required where the individual is evaluated by the event medic.

Any individual that exhibits one of the 'normal' signs of a concussion will be required to submit to regular checks by the medic during the day and will only be allowed to return to activity if the medic allows (This is because some of the symptoms may not necessarily be due to a concussion).

Any individual that exhibits 2 or more of the signs and symptoms of a concussion will be required to cease physical activity for the day. It should be heavily suggested that they see a physician for a checkup. Also, the medic should inform anyone who will be in close proximity of the individual for the next 24 hours to be alert for additional signs and what to do.

If at any time an individual shows any of the 'Danger' signs of a concussion, an ambulance should be called to have the individual taken for hospital evaluation.

These policies pertain to all Order martial activities, including but not limited to: live steel activities, soft sword activities, subjective rules activities (COKER RULES), field battles, games of skill such as Orc Ball, tournaments, practices, etc.

An incident report is required for ALL suspected or actual head injuries.

Medic Training

All persons wishing to serve as Order medics must complete this training and receive an appropriate authorization card. In the event no authorized medic is available, a knight herald may approve, for one event only, a medic with the following CURRENT state or federal issued licenses: Physician/MD. Physician's Assistant/PA. Nurse Practitioner/RNP. Registered Nurse/RN. Paramedic. Emergency Medical Technician/EMT.

Please require these personnel to complete the first responder application AND to read the following sections of the Rules of the Lyst before they begin service:
Section 1, subsections 11 through 14
Section 4
Section 10, subsections 4 and 5

Order Medical Officers (medics)

Appointment as an Order Medical Officer/Medic (sometimes referred to as a "surgeon" in the medieval colloquialism) is no small matter. Serious consideration should be given as to who is appropriate and who is not. A knight herald, the lord herald, a grand knight beacon and the SGKB may all appoint medics. ALL order medics, with the exception of special circumstances medics in the above section, are govern by these policies:

- Have a current state issued license for Physician/MD. Physician's Assistant/PA. Nurse Practitioner/RNP. Registered Nurse/RN. Paramedic. Emergency Medical Technician/EMT AND complete an Order first responder application and review the above listed sections of the ROTL.
- OR have one of the following current certifications: American Red Cross First Responder, BSA First Responder, Wilderness First Responder, state issued sports trainer certification, or similar level training AND complete the Order Concussion Policy Training, complete the first responder application, complete the below checklist, review the appropriate sections of the ROTL, AND be approved by the appropriate GKB.

KOFL Medic Team Authorization Card

Medic Name: _____

Training Level: _____

GKB Approval: Herald Approval:

Training Checklist for KOFL Medics

Completed the First Responder Application
      Initials/Date _____

Completed the CDC Concussion Awareness Training
      Initials/Date _____

Have current issued credentials
      Initials/Date _____

Has read the appropriate ROTL Sections
      Initials/Date _____

Understand and agree to the following additional policies
      Initials/Date _____

- Must at all times be engaged with the martial activity, alert and aware of action and what is going on at any time. Medics may NOT wear headphones nor be engaged in any activity other than monitoring the lyst field or combat activity while on duty.
- Medics must refrain from making or receiving phone calls while activity is happening.
- Medics must be familiar with all medical equipment and "jump bags" available. Medics will inventory gear before and after event and report any needs to knight or lord herald.
- Medics will complete, or cause to be completed, an incident report each and every time their services are required at an Order martial activity or meeting, and forward it to the appropriate authority.

Range Safety and Training

With the success of movies like The Hunger Games and Lord of the Rings, plus a recent focus at local schools, archery is a growing sport. As such, and traditionally, KOFL has an active archery program. Please follow the below safety rules. Heralds may consider appointing a range master for their chapter if they do any archery, otherwise the duty is theirs. The Order website has a FULL archery instructor training powerpoint presentation for review.

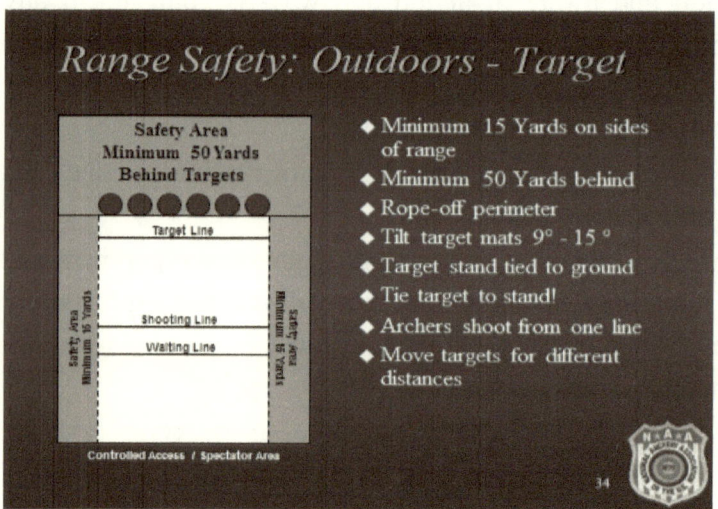

Outdoor ranges are the norm. Physical barriers such as walls or properly hung tarps can lesson the safety margins. The primary safety device however is a DISCIPLINED, WELL TRAINED AND CONSIENTIOUS range master.

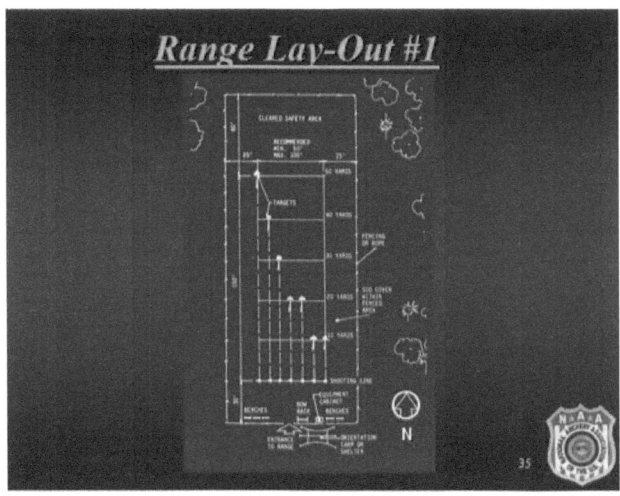

Standard outdoor shooting range. Note, when dealing with adult shooters, it is permissible to allow the target to remain static and the shooters retreat for longer ranges. But when feasible, change ranges by moving targets not shooters for safety. When shooters must move, ENSURE EACH AND EVERYTIME, that arrows are quivered before anyone

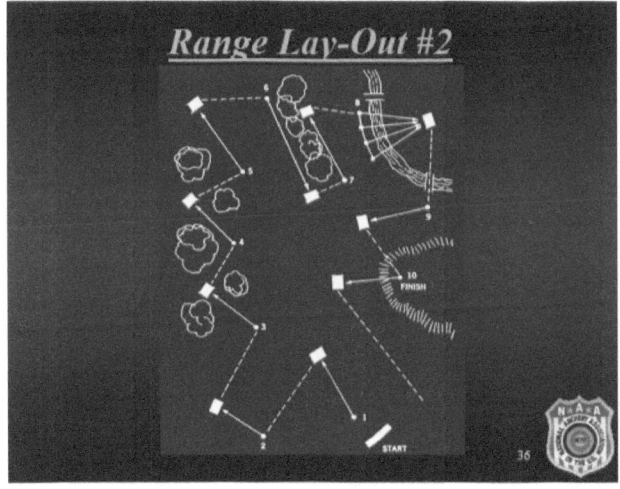

An example of a "combat" style course.

Range Supervision:

Age of Participants	# Students per Instructor
6-7 Years Old	2 or 3
8-9 Years Old	4 to 8
10-11 Years Old	8 to 12
12-15 Years Old	Up to 12
15 & up	12 to 20
Developmentally Disabled	May need 1 on 1

42

BSA Archery Safety Rules

- Always WALK on an Archery Range!
- Always Aim/Shoot at your designated Target!
- Always be Sure Area Around/Behind Target is Clear Before Shooting!
- Always Shoot at a Target Thick Enough to Stop Your Arrow!
- Always Use Proper Safety Equipment!
- Always Use Arrows of the Proper Length!
- Always Inspect Equipment Before Shooting!
- Always Wait for *"ALL CLEAR"* Command Before Retrieving Arrows!
- Always Lean Bow on Face of Target When Retrieving Arrows Behind it!
- Use a Field Captain If More Than 4 Archers Shoot or 1 Target is Used!
- Always Have an Arrow in the Bow Before Releasing the String!
- Always Shoot an Arrow at a Definite Target!

43

Archery Range Rules

◆ Know and obey all range commands

◆ Keep your arrows in your quiver until you are told to shoot

◆ Always wear an arm guard and finger tab

◆ Only use arrows that were given to you and remember what they look like

◆ Always keep your arrows pointed down or towards the target. Shoot only at your target

◆ Leave dropped arrows on the ground until told to retrieve arrows

◆ Always walk at the archery range

44

Archery Range Procedures

◆ Wait behind the waiting line until you hear 2 whistle blasts or "Archers to the shooting line." Pick up your bows and straddle the shooting line.

◆ Keep your arrows in your quiver until you hear 1 whistle blast or "Begin shooting."

◆ After you have shot all of your arrows, step back from the shooting line, set your bow on the rack, and wait behind the waiting line.

◆ After everyone is done shooting and behind the waiting line, the instructor will blow the whistle 3 times or say "Walk forward and get your arrows. Stop at the target line."

49

Line Judges

From the Rules of the Lyst 1.2: *"Any member of the Order of Man-at-Arms rank or better may be a Lyst Judge and are appointed by the Lyst Marshal for that combat(s).*
The Lyst Judge responsibilities include watching for any and all safety issues that may
come up during the combat, including but not limited to damaged or unsafe weapons and armor
and spectators and animals getting to close to the Lyst Field.
The Lyst Judge can call a "Hold" if any safety problems arise or if they KNOW they saw
a good hit.
Once a "Hold" is called by the Lyst Judge he will inform the Lyst Marshal why they
called the "Hold" by either saying the reason or using the hand signs.
If the Lyst Marshal calls the hold then the Lyst Judge will inform the Lyst Marshal of
what they have seen by either telling the Lyst Marshal or by using the hand signs.
Lyst Judges may also help the combatants and the Lyst Marshal with weapons, armor,
and water as needed."

Training standards for line judges are far less restrictive or comprehensive than Lyst Marshals. Basically, training consists of the line judge being able to properly demonstrate each and every signal required, and knowing the rules of the combat (IE seven point, etc.) Experience has demonstrated the following desirable characteristics of a line judge:

- Natural or corrected 20/20 vision.
- Experience in the lyst of at least six months. The more the better.
- Sound judgment, no history of favoritism or bias.
- Certified lyst marshals make excellent line judges.
- Loud voices that carry and project.

- Physically able to stand for periods of time.
- Good attention span.

There is no line judge certification or documentation required. Line judges do NOT have to be Order members, but do need to be experienced fighters in the style they are judging.

Line judges Lord Paul Satenstein, Sir James Morasso and Man-at-arms Johnathon McCartney judge a soft sword match between two Pages' Program maidens, Jasmine Shaver and Hayley Talley at the 2013 Viking Festival. His Grace Lord Karl Strohminger is heralding.

Care and Feeding of Live Steel

By His Grace Lord Michael Black

The Proper Care and Feeding of Armor and Weapons

This is a brief treatise on how to maintain metal armor and weapons commonly used within the medieval reenactment community. It is not meant to be all knowing or encompassing. It is derived strictly from the lessons I've learned over the last 22 years, both through formal training and self taught lessons, mostly learned the hard way. If you have something that works for you by all means keep doing it. If it ain't broke…. As a disclaimer I am not a metallurgist nor a professional armorsmith or weaponsmith. I am an enthusiast who has picked up some useful knowledge along the way. I hope this proves as useful to you as it has to me.

When maintaining armor and weapons it is vitally important to know what type of material you're working with. Metal has many forms. Cold steel, heat treated steel, spring steel, stainless steel, titanium, aluminum and so on. There are an inordinate number of alloys out there. We'll only be discussing a few here.

Cold Steel

Armor and weapons made from cold steel, which is steel that hasn't been exposed to extreme heat outside of its original production, is fairly predictable and if maintained properly can offer decades of service. It is also easy to produce and work with so it is fairly reasonably priced.

It is easily worked with and more malleable than heat treated steel and stainless steel. This means that you'll spend more time hammering dents out, but it isn't that hard. A hard surface like an anvil or quarter inch welding plate and a 16 oz. ball peen hammer will do just fine. Due to its softer nature it's very easy to drill holes for rivets too. Taking off burs with a metal file is also fairly simple. Just remember the cutting, drilling or filing rule: *measure twice and cut once. You can always take more off, but you can't put it back.*

Cold steel is quick to oxidize (rust) so keeping it clean is vital. For cleaning I use WD-40 and a 3M green scrub pad. For heavier rust or pitting I use a medium wire wheel on a standard 3/8ths hand drill. For quick cleanups of spotting I use a sponge sander. After cleaning I wipe it down with a towel and get all the debris off. Then it gets a very thin coat of RemOil. This is gun oil made by Remington. Some folks use metal polish or other wax based coating. Others used mineral oil or some form of petroleum based oil. Over the years I've found that RemOil works best because it has a Teflon component that helps prevent oxidation. You'll also use much less RemOil than other products. Just remember to wear latex style gloves when using any of these products as frequent and prolonged exposure may cause health issues.

Regarding paint, I like to keep the exterior of my armor an 'authentic' look. It is never polished to a high shine. It is dented, gouged, and has a rough brush finish at best. However, I keep the inside of my armor painted to save me maintenance time. Nobody sees it and it keeps you from having to clean your armor twice: once outside, once inside. Also, because of the athletic nature of reenactment the inside of armor rusts ten times faster than the outside because of exposure to sweat. So save yourself the angst and paint the inside of your armor. I use Rustoleum flat primer grey. It works and it's cheap. There are "high impact" paints out there but I've found they aren't worth the extra money.

Heat Treated Steel

Also known as forged steel or hot steel, it is steel that has been heated to extreme temperatures and cooled quickly to strengthen it. Heat treated steel is stronger and is often lighter and thinner than its cold counterpart. It is also more expensive as the production process is more involved. The finest armor and weapons in the world are heat treated steel. Nothing is finer and they come with the appropriate price tag.

Heat treated steel is harder, and therefore not as easy to work with as cold steel. It won't dent easily, but if it does you can still hammer it out. A good heavy anvil and ball peen hammers in a variety of weights and even a hand sledge may be necessary to get the job done. For drilling holes a drill press works best as it will give you extra leverage and control. Remember to use drill lubricant so you don't burn out the bit on the harder steel. For burs the steel file is still the best. Again, it is important to remember the cutting, drilling, or filing rule.

Heat treated steel is also quick to oxidize and I use the same regiment for it as I do for cold steel.

Stainless Steel

Ok, time to clear up a big misnomer. "Stainless" steel isn't stainless. It is stain *resistant*. It is essentially an alloy of cold steel and chromium that is heat treated. It has all the attributes of heat treated steel with the addition that it is very slow to oxidize. I maintain and work with stainless steel the same way I do heat treated steel only I have to do it $1/10^{th}$ as often. However, the more you 'work' stainless steel the faster it oxidizes. So the more it gets beat up and dents hammered out the faster it starts to rust.

In the appropriate gauge it is great for armor. It is, however, lousy for weapons. Stainless steel has the drawback of being more brittle than cold or heat treated steel and therefore is unsuitable for weapons other than pretty wall hangers.

Aluminum

Thanks to modern materials you can now have armor made from aluminum. Aluminum is great. It's lightweight, easy to work with and affordable. However, to provide the requisite protection for most reenactment groups it must be several gauges thicker than steel and is restricted for some pieces of armor. Aluminum is wholly unsuited for weapons other than 'wasters', which are literally single use sword analogs that are designed for a single training and demonstration.

I wouldn't wear aluminum armor less than 12 gauge (compared to cold steel at 16 gauge or heat treated steel at 18 gauge) because it just won't stand up to the beatings and quite frankly it isn't safe in my opinion. Its use should be limited to body protection. Even in heavy gauges aluminum doesn't make for a safe helm.

Maintaining aluminum is ridiculously easy. Aluminum oxidizes slower than cold or heat treated steel, and its 'rust' is white, not brown-orange. How do you clean it? Hot soapy water with a 3M scrub pad and towel dry. No kidding, that's it. Just like an aluminum pot or pan from the kitchen. I would still paint the insides for the same reasons as other metals. It saves maintenance time. Aluminum is also very easy to polish so if you like the 'knight in shining armor' look it's great. It can also be worn all day and you don't have to be an athlete to do it.

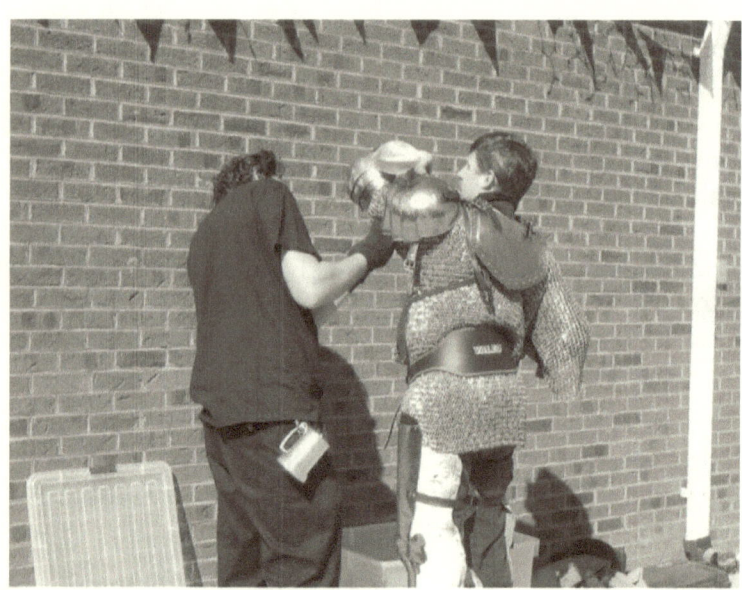

Sir Preston Absher getting ready for the Lyst with the assistance of Sir Kody Tench.

Section IV: Combat Rules

Over the years, KOFL members have come up with a variety of non-traditional combat styles and exciting games. This section details a preliminary basic set of rules for these games. When possible, the member responsible for the game or rules is cited for recognition, additional information or advice.

1) KOFL scoring.
   a. The traditional KOFL scoring system is an untimed seven point match. Points are awarded as such:
      i. Two points for head strikes (cuts only)
      ii. Three points for torso cuts, pulls and thrusts
      iii. One point for limb cuts, pulls and thrusts
      iv. Disarms allow for a point of honor for rearming or an automatic win (fighter's choice), A lyst marshal may award points of honor for other honorable acts, such as allowing an opponent to fix a broken piece of armor.
   b. However, nothing in the Rules of the Lyst prevents other scoring totals. Seven was selected because of historical references. Fights to 11 or 15 are common as are 5 point bouts. Pretty much, anything the fighters and lyst marshal deem appropriate are permissible. There are even fighters where the point threshold for victory is different for each fighter, a very fair way to equalize the match. (Fight-a-knight is an example.)
   c. Please see the Rules of the Lyst for full KOFL traditional bout and match rules.

2) Coker Rules

The Coker Rules

By His Grace Lord Michael Black, PMM

I. Purpose:
This is an effort to create a form of live steel competition, functioning as an addendum to the existing KOFL Rules of the Lyst (see Articles of Organization, Appendices), to replace the controversial form of combat known as "To the Yield". This will create a fun, aggressive form of elevated live steel combat in a well-regulated process with safety at its core.

II. Form:
The Coker Rules will mirror greatly the rules that regulate the participation in and judging of boxing and mixed martial arts matches.

III. Rules:
    A. Format –
        1. Duration - Each contest will consist of three rounds of at least thirty seconds in duration each. Duration may be longer based on conditions and combatant agreement. I.E. Combatant X wants the rounds to be 1 minute in duration and Combatant Y agrees to the change.
        2. Rest Periods - A rest period of no less than four times the duration of the round will occur in between rounds. Rest periods may be longer based on conditions and combatant agreement. I.E. Combatant X is being tested for his Feat of Combat using Coker rules and requires longer rest periods in between rounds. This is agreed upon by the combatants, chapter Knight Herald, and reviewing Heartsman prior to the start of the Feat.
        3. Timekeeper - There must be a designated official timekeeper with an appropriate functioning

chronometer with minute and second capacity. The clock starts at "LAY ON" and continues until "HOLD". Counting a combatant out (10 count), a standing 8 count (as part of a technical knockout), or other reasons for the marshal stopping the round are done off the clock. A combatant being counted out cannot be "saved by the bell".

4. Combatants - Two combatants will fight each contest. Combatants must meet or exceed the weapons and armor safety requirements as explained in the Rules of the Lyst version 1.2.

5. Rounds - When the contest is begun with the marshal's command "LAY ON" the combatants will engage and continue fighting until the round time duration has expired. When "HOLD" is called the combatants will disengage and remove to their prospective corners of the lyst field for the rest period. At the end of the rest period the combatants will re-engage with the command "LAY ON" and repeat the process until the contest is complete or "HOLD" is called.

6. Victory – Victory is achieved in one of five ways: knockout, technical knockout, marshal stoppage, yielding, and judges' decision.

   a. Knockout – Defined as the loss of consciousness, the combatant being non-responsive for a duration of no less than three seconds and/or going to their knees or lower and being unable to stand within a 10 count (which is done with the clock stopped).

   b. Technical Knockout – Defined as a combatant going to their knees or lower two times throughout the entire contest, or being disarmed or being unable to perform a mandatory standing eight count after the first such occurrence of either.

   c. Marshal Stoppage – Defined as the marshal on the lyst field determining that a combatant is not or cannot actively defend themselves, a combatant's required armor is damaged and they cannot carry on according to safety guidelines, they are injured and/or physically unfit for combat (the marshal must have first responder advice for this) or a deliberate or negligent rule violation is committed by a combatant.

d. Yielding – Defined as a combatant, or his designee (a designee is not required), deciding he cannot continue and ending the contest.

e. Judges' Decision – Defined as a victor being chosen by way of scored rounds (see Article III, paragraph C, section 1.)

B. Marshaling - One marshal will control each contest. The marshal will be in the lyst field with the combatants and be suitably armed and armored so that he may execute the duties of his charge. This should include at a minimum an open faced full helm, gorget, gauntlets and sport cup. The marshal is responsible for lyst field and combatant safety. He may not award points or in any other way decide the conclusion of a contest outside his prerogatives (see Article III, paragraph A, section 6, subparagraph c). The marshal will call "HOLD" for the end of a round; breaking up combatants entangled for at least 5 seconds, a combatant goes to their knees or lower, a disarming, weapon or armor malfunction, or any other safety concern.

C. Judging - Each contest will be judged by three judges, none of which may be the marshal or timekeeper. The judges will follow the regulations of scoring.

1. Scoring - Each round is scored individually based on the **3 Point System**. That is to say 3 points are awarded per judged category, in every round. The categories are as follows: *strike quantity* (number of clean strikes to legal targets of sufficient force), *strike effectiveness*, *defense (shield work/parrying)*, *lyst field control* and *aggression*. The number of points awarded in each category is

based on the performance of the combatants. For example, if combatant X lands **slightly** more strikes than combatant Y then the relative strike quantity score would be 2/1. If combatant X lands a **clearly dominant** number of strikes than combatant Y then the relative strike quantity score would be 3/0. No half points may be awarded. If a Knockout or Technical Knockout occur that round is not scored. The scores of the judges are combined to form a Round Score. The Round Scores are combined to form a Contest Score. The Contest Score is used to decide the victor in a Judges' Decision victory.

2. Disarming – If a combatant is disarmed of their weapon, and they are not in possession of another, then the marshal will call "HOLD". The disarmed combatant must complete a standing 8 count after rearming. If they complete it the contest continues and the disarming is counted as either the first or second part of a Technical Knockout depending on the circumstances. If they cannot complete the standing 8 count then the contest ends (see Article III, Section A, Paragraph 6, subsection b Technical Knockout).

3. Documentation – Judges must use the official Coker Rules Scorecard to score each contest. Completed scorecards will be kept on file by the Chapter Knight Herald for local events and Lord Herald for grand events.

His Grace Lord Michael Black, author of the Coker Rules, takes a break between wins.

3) Dagorhir KOFL adapted rules
    a. The Fiat Lux has a close association with the Dagorhir Battle Games national organization. As such, there are often times when our two organizations overlap. When attending a Dagorhir event, KOFL members are obligated to learn and follow the rules of that community, lengthy as they are. A full set of those rules can be downloaded at http://www.dagorhir.com/index.php/rules/printer-friendly-version

    b. There are events where KOFL hosts or presents field battle type scenarios as well. Naughty Hamm is a good example. KOFL has adopted the following adapted Dagorhir rules for those events. Full acknowledgement and appreciation to Dagorhir for their willing license to our organization is given. These adapted rules are designed to be as simple to learn and use as possible while maintaining safety and historical logic. (Lord Karl Strohminger created these adapted rules with assistance by Sir James Reithmiller and Lord Paul Satenstein.)

        i. Hits.

            1. Cuts, thrusts and strikes by a bladed weapon to any limb results in the limbs "severing". Drop any object you are holding with that limb or take a knee accordingly. Any two limb severs equals death.

2. Cuts, thrusts and strikes of any nature to the torso results in death.
3. Cuts and strikes to the head result in death.
4. Blunted strikes to limbs result in the limb being unusable but do not kill. IE, a flail or mace could disable every limb but the fighter survives, vulnerable as he is then.
5. Arrows and bolts. Operate just as a "red" bladed weapon. (see below)
6. Javelins and thrown weapons. Operate just as a "green" weapon (see below) with one exception. Full plate armor is invulnerable to any small thrown hand weapon (hammers, axes, knives, rocks, darts, etc) but not javelins.
7. Siege engines. Kill on contact, period. Large siege engines (trebuchet, catapults) kill on contact AND within a five foot radius, period.

ii. Armor
1. Leather armor (of ROTL permissible grade) provides one additional level (point) of protection per match or battle ONLY on areas covered. IE, if a torso has a leather breast

plate, but the back does not, the back is NOT protected.

2. Chain provides two levels/points of protection.
3. Metal plate provides three.
4. Non-standard plate materials (like plastic) provide two.
5. Armor may "stack" (combine) up to three levels.
6. Armor loses one level/point (or two for red weapons) every time it is struck.

iii. Weapons

1. Weapons have level values (points) as well. The math is easy. Any total in excess of the armor level value deals damage.

   a. Green weapons – are thrusting. IE they have a stab point. Spears, most swords, daggers, darts, etc. 1 pt.
   b. Blue weapons are one handed blades like a long sword or axe. 1 pt.
   c. Red weapons deal two points of damage and must be wielded with two hands. Red weapons wielded with one hand only do blue damage. Two handed

swords and polearms are two types. 2 pts.

d. Yellow weapons are one handed blunt, like a flail. They do one point. 1 pt.

e. Combinations: red/green and blue/green are allowed.

4) Roundrobins and Bear Pits – two popular lyst variations are Roundrobin and Bear Pit events and tournaments. (Lord Karl uses these rules often at Chivalry Sports Academy.)

a. Roundrobins are basically events or tournaments whereby every fighter fights every other fighter a predetermined number of times in whichever fight style is desired (seven point, Coker, etc).

b. Bear Pits come to us from the Society of Creative Anachronism and can be one of the most fun, if grueling, combat experiences one can have. The lyst marshal selects one fighter to "own the field" (starts). Often the selection is by seniority, or some other veteran status. That fighter then faces off against all other fighters in the queue until he loses. Again, any style may be used. Once the starting fighter (and/or subsequent winners) loses, he gets in the back of the queue for his next chance. The winner is he who has the longest win streak.

5) Games

a. Orc Ball (written by Sir Gene Kinney)

General Information

Orc ball is a very entertaining game that can be enjoyed by anyone. All ages may play, and it is very easy to learn, play and excel. It can be played by as little as 4 people, with as many as 30 and is a great competitive sports version of KOFL sports and martial training.

NOTE: All general rules will be formatted to the 10 person total teams as that is most frequently the case. Following chapters will advise on how to adjust for players.

Equipment

Because ORC BALL follows the official KOFL Rules of the Lyst 1.2, ALL players MUST have the following:

- Standard Sports Cup (males)
- ROTL Approved Weapon
- Sturdy Footwear
- Approved Helm

Now, the Following is either suggested, or optional:

- Knee/Elbow pads
- ROTL approved Shield/Javelin/Other Misc. weapon
- Any Armor (non-metal)
- Regalia (Makes for a VERY fun match)
- Flags (In lieu of weapons)

The Following Equipment is REQUIRED for the field:

- Soft Ball/Skull to be the Orc Ball (IE Nerf ball)
- Ropes or other signifying device for boundaries

The Following Equipment is Suggested or Optional for the Field:

- Catapult/Trebuchet

- Vests to signify teams

A big note about the equipment: the more fun you have setting up the game the more fun you will have. Sure, 6 guys playing the game is fun but if you have a Catapult the shoot the ball, with 3 guys in tusks catching it and charging down the field with a howl.... Now that's even more fun.

Rules of the Lyst

SAFETY is the number one priority. The following rules are enforced.
- ANY player/coach/bystander/referee that calls HOLD WILL be obeyed immediately
- The designated Referee (Honor system works in small groups) is the Marshall. His word is LAW
- Team Captains are effectively Line Judges for his/her team. They may call to any member of THEIR team out. Again, honor trumps all
- Sufficient force will be followed (Age/Experience relative)
- If you are hit with sufficient force YOU ARE OUT. Proceed to the dead box immediately.
- Any player found in violation of the rules will receive ONE penalty for 2 minutes of game time (Stops in between plays do not run the clock). Second Violation is benched.
- If there is a dispute about a play it will be settled by the designated Referee. If there is no dedicated referee Team Captains will decide among themselves.
- If you run out of bounds play STOPS immediately.
- The Designated Referee may at any time institute FAIR and LEGAL rules as he sees fit as long as: Safety is observed, and Both Team Captains are in Agreement.
- Please refer to your specific section about what rules come into play with larger/smaller parties.
- A Qualified Medical person WILL be on site
- DOWNS: (like in American Football) are called when:
  ○ The Orc Ball carrier is struck by an opponent's weapon (Refer to Armor rules for supplement)

○   ANY Elbow, hand, or Knee that touches the ground by the Orc Ball carrier

•   At any Change of Possession (Offensive Turnover, COP play, etc.) all players are returned to life

Gameplay

The Different positions in the game mean different things based on the number of people. Positions listed MUST be specified before any offensive unit begins a possession. Changes may be made with the exception of the Captain and Healer position. The following are the names:

Offense

Tank – Think Lineman with Shields

Healer – Optional rule for smaller teams. May heal "Wounds" on a five count

Captain – The Quarterback

Thief – Running Back

Striker – Generally just goes and kills things

Defense

Safety – Generally covers the deep zone

Corner – Covers the sides

Blitz – Up front, rushes the Captain

Captain – Runs the Defense

Healer – See above

The Field usually should extend 100 feet lengthwise, 50 feet width, With a 15 foot End zone at each end. Different specs for smaller groups are permitted. It should be roped off, or have cones/markers designating out of bounds, beginning and end of the end zone, and one for the Line of Scrimmage. Orc Ball should NEVER be played on a hard surface in any capacity larger than 6 total players.

Basic rules are below. If you think of Ultimate Frisbee combined with Football and Rugby, in the 10th century, you have Orc Ball.

Each player should carry a weapon, with even teams. Kickoff will go to the winner of a coin toss (Or similar selection method) The Kicking team must loft the ball to their opponent, either by hand or Catapult. The Receiver may signal a Fair Catch by waving his arm visibly in the air before reception occurs. This means that NO Defender may hit him and must provide at LEAST 5 feet of room for the catch to be made. In return, the receiver may not move from the spot of reception, and their set of downs will begin on that spot. IF the receiver DOES NOT touch the ball, any opposing player that touches the ball immediately downs it at that spot for the receiving team to take over. Otherwise, the receivers may elect to not signal a safe reception, and let the battle take it where it will.

SHOULD the Kickoff Returner touch, and DROP the ball, and the Kicking team recovers it, then they now have possession at the site of down.

IF the Kick or Throw goes out of bounds laterally, (As in the sides of the field) the ball is down at the exact spot it went out of bounds. If it goes out of bounds in regards to the back of the end zone then it is a touchback, and moves out 20 feet from the end zone. Alternatively, any kickoff that is received in the end zone (And not moved into the end zone), the Receiver may take a knee and receive a touchback

During Play, Each team is allowed a 30 second huddle to decide their formation. Once the Line of Scrimmage (The spot where the ball begins before play) is determined, no team may cross to the opponents side until the Offensive Captain calls "Hike" which signals the begin of play.
(Refer to 2v2 play for supplement rules in this situation)

The Offensive team may then do any of the following:
- Perform a Run play
- Perform a Pass Play
- Perform a Change of Possession play
- Perform a Trick play

With a Run Play, the Captain MUST hand or pitch the ball to his Runner. The pitch MUST BE either PARALLEL or BEHIND the line of scrimmage. A Forward Pitch will be penalized. The Runner may then: Run with the ball over the Line of Scrimmage, or choose to throw the ball. The Runner MUST be behind the line of scrimmage in order for him to throw forward, and his target must ALSO have crossed the line. A Forward Lateral will be penalized.

With a Pass Play the Captain may choose to attempt to throw the ball to a receiver on his team. A Receiver may be any other player (Supplemental rules excluded). Receivers DO NOT need to be designated as such before play begins. The Receiver must have a free hand, and must make a successful catch with one, or two hands. He must have full possession of the ball before being downed, or else the pass is incomplete.

A Defender, however, may attempt to intercept, or deflect the pass. To catch he must have a free hand. THE SAME RULE applies to defenders attempting to intercept. Violation will result in an Offensive Pass Interference penalty being called. The two Receivers (Offensive and Defensive) may attempt to block each other's chances of catching (Soft nudging, hand in front of eyes, etc.) but any hard shove that causes one party to fall will be Pass Interference.

A Change of Possession Play is any play where the Offensive team willingly relinquishes possession of the ball to their opponent. Such can be done by: Throw off, Bloodbath, Or a Throw up. The Offensive team MUST inform the defenders of their intention for a COP (out) play.

A Throw off is a standard punt play. The Captain must throw the ball as far as he can to an opposing receiver who will then catch and take possession. A Fair Catch may be signaled. Follow standard Kickoff rules for specifics.

A Bloodbath is a COP play that may only be used with 10+

people playing. What happens is the Offense takes a 10 foot penalty, with the Line of Scrimmage not changing (As in, there is now 10 feet between the Defenders and the Offense, but the technical spot of the ball is at the Offenders). Then, each Offensive player receives one extra HBD (Hit Before Down) The Ball is handed to the referee (Allowing the Captain one extra hand to use) and 'Hike' is called. Both teams goal, is to slay every member of their opponent's team. There are no respawns. Whatever side succeeds takes over possession, with a new set of downs, at the current spot of the ball. Running out of Bounds will result in the death of the player that stepped out. At the end of a Bloodbath all players return to life.

A Throw Up may be used in any case where a Throw Off will result in a touchback for sure. The teams both drop their weapons and form two semi circles around the Referee. The Ref then throws the ball as straight and as high as he can. Whichever team is downed with possession of the ball earns 2 downs. The spot of the ball may not move from the spot of downing.

A Trick Play is any play that a team may do that does not follow the current format of plays. Examples of such are:
Receiver Reverse plays- (Where the runner is handed the ball, and then hands it off to another receiver who runs in the opposite direction)

Trick Throw off Play – This is the only COP play that may be faked. The Captain of the Offensive team MUST inform the Referee in private that he intends a fake. The Ref then measures a 10 foot distance from the line of Scrimmage that the offense MUST cross for new downs.

Bedbug flicker – Where the Runner is handed the ball, pitches it back to the Captain, who then throws it downfield.

Teams are encouraged to think of trick plays to use as long as they are LEGAL.

Size Specific Rules

The Following rules supplement the above for any match that has 4-8 total players:
- The Field SHOULD be reduced to a size appropriate in the eyes of the Ref
- Each team gets 4 downs to score. If, at the end of 4, they haven't scored, the defense gets possession.
- Bloodbath COP may not be attempted
- Each player only needs to receive one hit before being out.
- The Healer position should be filled.
- Tanks receive nothing special
- At any 'Hike' the Defense must count OUT LOUD to '5 Mississippi' before crossing the Line of Scrimmage to down the ball. If the ball crosses the line at any points (Even if it goes back) the Defense may immediately go after the ball.
- At every new down all players Regenerate
- Each game will last appx. 30 minutes (At the leisure of the Ref) or until one team has 3 points

The Following rules supplement the above for any match that has 10-16 total players:
- The Field should be kept at the standard, 100x50 size. If the Ref believes that the field should be changed he may do so.
- The Tank Position may only be filled to a Ratio of 1:5 for each team.
- Tanks Are NOT allowed to carry the ball. HOWEVER they receive 5 total HBD (Hits Before Down) per set of downs. After those 5 are extinguished they are dead permanently until change of possession. The Captain may not be the Tank.
- Players must proceed to the Dead Box for their team until a total of two players (Excluding a Tank) then the player in there the longest comes back into play.
- If the Captain is in the Dead box at the start of a down, another team mate shall be designated as such until he is back in

the game.
- Any Armor worn may be classified as such:
  - Light Armor (Leather, Light Chain Maille, Brigandine) = 1 Extra HBD
- The Healer May not wear ANY armor, or Carry the ball. He also may not carry anything other than a single, one handed weapon. There is only one per team.
- The Healer has a few special options. First, Once per down he may place his hand on a recently dead team mate and bring him back to life. Immediately. Second, Once per set of downs, He may sacrifice his life to re-do the play. Doing so will remove him permanently from play until his team gets possession once more (As in, they have lost possession since his death, been on defense, and recovered the ball again). He does not count toward the Dead Box total if he has done this. And third, a Defensive Healer may ALSO sacrifice himself the same way an Offensive one will in order to counteract the Offense's sacrifice. Doing so allows the Defense to have the turnover still, but the Defensive Healer is removed from play for the next two possessions (As in, His team has had the ball once, and the opponents have had it once, as soon as the ball comes back to his team a second time he comes back to life). During a Bloodbath, a Healer becomes a regular fighter. If he was dead beforehand, he will regenerate for that down only, and then return to permanently dead status after. A Healer MAY NOT reverse a Turnover due to a COP play or expiration of downs
- The team does not need a Healer.
- Game plays for appx. 60 minutes (At the decision of the Ref), or until one team has 5 points.
- Each team Gets 4 Downs, but if they travel a distance specified by the Ref from the first Line of Scrimmage (Usually 15 feet) they get One extra down
- One Referee is Required

The Following rules supplement the above for any match that has 18-30 total players:
- The Field should be expanded to 120 feet – 200 feet length, and 80-100 width.

- Tanks Follow the Same Restrictions as above EXCEPT they follow a 1:7 Ratio, are given 7 Points of life per set of downs, and can wear NO armor.
- A Team may have NO MORE than two Healers on their team.
- Tanks Must carry a Shield
- Runners MAY NOT carry a shield
- A team may have as many Strikers as they wish but they may not carry the ball unless no one on their team is left alive.
- The Dead box will hold 4 Team Mates. Once a 5th one is killed the next eligible one spawns. (Not counting Tanks, or Permanently dead Healers)
- A team MUST travel 20 feet from the start of their downs in order to earn more. They have 4 chances to do so. ALTERNATIVLY the Referee, with the agreement of the Captains at the beginning of play, may choose to play '6 Hard' in which the players may NEVER earn more downs (Including Bloodbath or Throw up). At the end of 6 the Defense takes over at the last spot of down.
- Game Plays for appx 100 minutes or until one Team has scored 7 points.
- A stoppage of time will be made EVERY 25 minutes for at least 5.
- There must be AT LEAST 2 Referee's. 3-4 is preferable.

Alternate Game Modes
0 Stop.
- In which play doesn't stop until a score is made.
◦ Any time the ball touches the ground the opposing team takes possession.
◦ If a player is killed while in possession of the ball he must throw it into the air immediately.
◦ To respawn you move to the designated area, call out "I AM NOW BACK IN THE FIGHT" and you may return to the game.
◦ Stops are made ONLY for Safety and Score.
◦ Special Positions do not exist
◦ Play continues for 30-45 minutes. Winning team is the one with the most points

Throw it up, Muck it up

•   In which each team has only one down to score

○   Very similar to the 0 Stop game mode except each down, your opponent kicks/throws/launches the ball to your end zone, and you have to make it to the opposing end zone that down to score.

○   If your opponent forces a turnover (Interception, Fumble, etc) they may in turn run it the opposite way for 2 points.

○   Any time the Defense makes a successful stop, they receive a point.

○   As soon as the ball touches the ground (Because of a killing, not because of a fumble) play ends. Players switch sides.

○   Play continues for 30-45 minutes.

○   There is no respawn during possession

     b) **European Orc Ball**   - (Lord Paul Satenstein)
     - European Orc Ball is NOT for the faint of heart. It combines soccer and traditional Orc Ball and is a heart racing fast pace game of athletic and martial prowess. It is considerably easier than Orc Ball however. Just play soccer with the addition of predetermined "time outs" for being killed (5 seconds, 30, 60 etc.). It is also recommended that Adapted Dagorhir rules of limb strikes be used.

     c) Battle Chess – Battle chess is NOT what you see on Harry Potter. Two players play a traditional game of chess on a chess board. Each piece is assigned a real fighter analogue and the square is awarded via who wins a traditional seven point match in the lyst. Alternatively, a three contact scoring may be uses (first to strike three times, no holds called). All other chess rules apply. Battle Chess was created at the Naughty Hamm by Lord Paul Satenstein.

     - The Chess pieces have the following weapons:

       - Pawns – long sword

- Knights – sword and shield

- Rooks – two handed swords

- Bishops – mace or quarterstaff

- Queen – poison dagger (kills on a single contact)

- King - dagger

D) King's Chess – This is what you think of when you think "Wizards Chess" from Harry Potter. The game plays as a regular chess game requiring a HUGE chess board on the ground with each square no less than 3x3 foot. Each piece is armed as above. Squares awarded either by the first three touches or a five point match. Play continues as regular chess with traditional movement, etc.   Adaption: Queen gets first strike missile weapons. Thanks to the Charlotte Chapter for this game!

E) The Gauntlet – Have you ever seen American Gladiator, Wipe Out or X-Factor? That's the Gauntlet! Each fighter must face a series of physical stunts, challenges, puzzles, combats, etc. in a timed course. Winner has the fastest time. Five second penalties for failing any challenge apply.   Challenges include, but are not limited to: physical stunts such as a balance beam, soldier craw, tunnel, tire step, climbing ropes or equipment, etc.; combat challenges of any type; archery; bravery tests (will he really drink that?); ethical puzzles often based on the Code; and anything else a course director can think of. Sir Franklin Fite first gave us this great game at the Second Annual Business Meeting in 2007. The Grand Strand Chapter bases an entire event (Big Beach Boffer Bash and Boil) on it.

F) King's Challenge Lyst – Simply put, the King's Challenge Lyst limits weapons choices per the Herald's (or some other leader's) discretion.   For example, the King's Challenge Lyst may allow free choice for the first round, sword and dagger for second fight, sword only for third, spears only, etc. etc. Historical Medieval Battles (AKA Battle of the Nations) uses a similar form for their one on one tournaments. Sir Gene Kinney created this challenging and advanced game.

G) Gladiator Games – Gladiator Games are a creation of Lord Karl's Chivalry Sports Academy. There are several.

o Two v. two – four fighters in the lyst at a time, teams of two. The only difference than a standard seven point match is instead of scoring points for hitting your opponent, you loose them for getting hit. This game requires at least one line judge per fighter to help with scoring. When a fighter gets to ZERO he leaves the field.
o Optional adaption – no holds are called upon someone being hit.
o Tag Team – Just like it sounds. Teams of two (or more) fight one at a time, and may "tag" (hand to hand only) out at any time except during a hold. Scoring works as in 2v2.
  i. Optional adaption - no holds called
o Non standard teams – as per 2v2 but any number.
o Ogre – one combatant is the "ogre" with a higher level of points (usually 11 or 15) and he faces off against 2 or more opponents. Scoring works as in 2v2 above.
  ii. Optional adaption – tag team version.
o Thunderdome – This is a game based on the hit Mad Max movie of the same name. Fighters are often lashed together (with a silk scarf, soft cuffs, etc.) and a single weapon is available with which to fight. Much wrestling, hilarity, entanglements, etc. ensue until one gets weapon and hits opponent. Lyst Marshal often throws in additional weapons as round progresses. Once the bind comes off, it stays off. Note, requires a padded or soft ground.

Other Resources - Bibliography

Satenstein, Paul, David Lazenby, Buck Holmes, and Preston Absher. *The Rules of the Lyst 1.2*. 1st ed. Vol. 1. Charlotte: Knightly Order of the Fiat Lux, NC. Print.

Strohminger, Karl, Ph.D., ed. *Knightly Order of the Fiat Lux Membership Handbook*. 1st ed. Vol. 1. Charlotte: Knightly Order of the Fiat Lux, NC. Print.

Veirling, David. "Dagorhir.com - Welcome to Dagorhir Battle Games." *Dagorhir.com - Welcome to Dagorhir Battle Games*. N.p., 2013. Web. 13 Jan. 2014.

Satenstein, Paul, Morasso, James. "Knightly Order of the Fiat Lux." *Home*. Knightly Order of the Fiat Lux, 10 Jan. 2014. Web. 13 Jan. 2014.

Black, Michael. *Care and Feeding of Metal Weapons and Armor*. Tech. 1st ed. Vol. 1. N.p.: n.p., n.d. Print.

Strohminger, Karl, Ph.D., Gene Kinney, and Jonathan McCartney. *KOFL Pages' Program*. 1st ed. Vol. 3. N.p.: Knightly Order of the Fiat Lux, 2103. Print.

"Starfire Forge." *Starfire Swords*. N.p., n.d. Web. 13 Jan. 2014. <http://starfireswords.com/info/home.php>.

Satenstein, Paul. "Naughty Hamm Planning." Personal interview. 25 Oct. 2013.

Kinney, Gene. "King's Challenge Planning." Personal Interview, 10 Nov. 2013.

www.ingramcontent.com/pod-product-compliance
Lightning Source LLC
Chambersburg PA
CBHW020401290526
45785CB00005B/2397